Bloody Elle

A Gig Musical

Written and Performed by
Lauryn Redding

The first performance of
Bloody Elle – A Gig Musical
was at the Royal Exchange Theatre, Manchester
on 23 June 2021

Bloody Elle

A Gig Musical

Elle	Lauryn Redding
Director	Bryony Shanahan
Designer	Amanda Stoodley
Sound Designer and Additional Composition	Alexandra Faye Braithwaite
Lighting Designer	Mark Distin Webster
Movement Director	Yandass Ndlovu
Dramaturg	Suzanne Bell
Associate Director	Hannah Sands
English BSL Interpreter	Siobhán Rocks
Audio Description	Anne Hornsby
Company Stage Manager	Scott McDonald
Deputy Stage Manager	Amber Chapell
Production Manager	Richard Delight
Producer	Katie Vine (for Royal Exchange) and Peter Holland (for Rebel Productions)

Writer's Note

Writing *Bloody Elle – A Gig Musical* been my light thru the dark.

I hope my words can do the same for you – take care of your lovely hearts.

Big love and bottomless thanks to Bryony Shanahan, Alexandra Faye Braithwaite, Peter J Holland, Hannah Sands, Suzanne Bell, Amanda Stoodley, Mark Distin Webster, Amber Chapell, Yandass Ndlovu, Siobhán Rocks and Scott McDonald.

For your belief. Your passion. Your hearts.

Thank you. For it all.

And a huge big ta to:

Emma Powell
Janet Gillison
Rachel Bunce
Douglas Runtoul
Anna Hunscott
Tom Jackson Greaves
Roy Alexander Weise
Cathy Crabb
James Frewer
Howard Coggins
Stu Mcloughlin
Adam Leonard-Burn
Andrew Mills
Rebecca Killick
Milky Sadler

Donna Preston
Rupert Hill
Pat Burbridge
Stephanie Martin
Kerry Whelan
Adam Lenson
Lotte Wakeham
Rob Waddington
Katie Vine
Steven Basket
Phil Costello
Stuart Mitchell
Felicia Jagne
Owen Lewis
And everyone at the Royal Exchange Theatre, Manchester

Director's Note

Working on a new piece is always special. Knowing that the entire team is creating something that's never been seen before is one of the best feelings as a director. It takes muscle and delicacy and bravery and also a load of faith from everyone involved!

But with this particular piece at this particular time, that sense of preciousness, of treasuring every moment together in the rehearsal room, of trying to bring this new, breathing, living thing to life, is intensified and is even more of a privilege than ever before.

Bloody Elle – A Gig Musical will be the first piece in the Royal Exchange Theatre in Manchester for fourteen months after the closures brought about due to the Covid-19 pandemic. It will be the first time audiences are welcomed through our doors again, dressing rooms will be occupied, machinery will be whirring, lights will focus on human beings, sound will land in the ears of those gathered together. There will be a first beginners' call, a first standby and (hopefully!) a first curtain call. The pandemic has been devastating for the entire world, and our industry has really suffered. Coming together for a live experience is what we do. We've had to think differently, find new ways of working, and have all faced the very real crisis of what happens if recovery isn't possible. But as opening gets closer and closer, that intangible but very real sense of excitement, and of preparing to share this story with strangers and friends, is starting to once more ignite a collective energy and a hopeful stride towards better times. So yeah, this one feels doubly special, and I'm sure is something none of us will forget.

It's also an odd thought, but despite us all being surrounded by so much loss and devastation at the hands of the virus, this piece actually wouldn't have been made if it weren't for these set of peculiar circumstances. The enforced time away from performing as well as other events landing simultaneously, meant that Lauryn had the time and somehow found the motivation to put pen to paper, and carve out Elle and all of the people that occupy her world. That's not to say any of us are glad this has happened, but it's nice to focus on a small piece of joy and I feel very grateful to her for creating something that is getting us back together again. As Elle is described in the play, 'life was tough, she was tougher, when life got rough, she got rougher'. I think this perfectly describes Lauryn over the past twelve months.

We're nothing without our colleagues, collaborators, audiences and participants. And I'm surrounded by brilliant people. There are too many to mention, but it takes a village. Thank you to every single one of you. To be heralding in a new era that I hope is full of joy, resilience and growth, with a piece that talks about love, endeavour and being exactly who you are in this world, and that is jam packed with beautiful songs and rousing music... feels right.

Lastly, in relation to this story in particular, no one says it better than Audre Lorde, so I'll leave it with her words: 'You do not have to be me in order for us to fight alongside each other.'

Bryony Shanahan
Director of *Bloody Elle – A Gig Musical*
Joint Artistic Director of Royal Exchange Theatre

Lauryn Redding (Writer & Performer)

Theatre credits include: *The Worst Witch* (Vaudeville Theatre, West End – Olivier Award winner); *The Hired Man* (Queen's Theatre, Hornchurch/Hull Truck/Oldham Coliseum); *Macbeth*/A *Midsummer Night's Dream/Twelfth Night* (Wilton's Music Hall); *Seagulls* (Bolton Octagon); *Oliver Twist* (Hull Truck); *Educating Rita* (UK Tour); *Bread and Roses/Up 'n' Under/Oh! What a Lovely War/Dreamers* (Oldham Coliseum); *Romeo and Juliet* (The Watermill Theatre); *Horrible Histories* (The Lowry); *The Comedy of Errors* (Shakespeare's Globe and UK/European Tour); *Treasure Island/Peter Pan in Scarlet* (New Vic Theatre); *Frankenstein* (Salisbury Playhouse); *An August Bank Holiday Lark/ She Stoops to Conquer/The Winter's Tale* (Northern Broadsides); *Alice's Adventures Underground* (Waterloo Vaults); *Barmy Britain/Barmy Britain Part Two – Horrible Histories* (Garrick Theatre, West End, UK and Australian tour); *Wind in the Willows* (West Yorkshire Playhouse); *King Lear/Different Buttons* (Red Rose Chain); *The Enough Project* (The Lowry); *Shhh* (Theatre503); *Numb* (Arcola Theatre); *Tall Tales* (Theatr Clywd).
Television credits include: *EastEnders* (BBC) *Emmerdale* (ITV); *Lee Nelson's Well Good Show* (BBC Three); *Regulars* (Channel 4).

Bryony Shanahan (Director)

Bryony Shanahan is Joint Artistic Director of the Royal Exchange Theatre. In 2016 she won the Genesis Future Directors Award and directed *Trade* at the Young Vic. During the past twelve months as Artistic Director she has developed projects such as *All I Want For Christmas* and *Oh Woman!* for the Royal Exchange. Her directing credits for the theatre include *Wuthering Heights*, *Adieu*, *Queens of the Coal Age* and *Nothing* (winner of Manchester Theatre Award). Other directing credits include *Enough* (Traverse Theatre); *Chicken Soup* (Sheffield Crucible); *Operation Crucible* (Finborough Theatre/Sheffield Crucible/UK tour/59e59 New York); *Weald* (Finborough Theatre); *Bitch Boxer* (Soho Theatre/national tour/Adelaide Fringe Festival); *Boys Will Be Boys* (Women Centre Stage, National Theatre); *Chapel Street* (national tour) and *You and Me* (Greenwich Theatre/national tour).

Amanda Stoodley (Designer)

Amanda is an award-winning set and costume designer, working in theatre, opera, installation and exhibition. She trained at Liverpool Institute for Performing Arts and graduated in 2009 with a First Class Honours degree in theatre and performance design. Amanda previously studied and worked in illustration, graphic, interior and stained-glass design. Credits include: *Queen Margaret*, *Moments That Changed Our World*, *Hamlet*, *Black Roses* (& UK Tour); *All I Want is One Night* (& Wilton's Music Hall); *Two*, *Winterlong* (& Soho Theatre); *Truth About Youth* Festival, *Making an Exhibition of Ourselves* (*At Home*) (Royal Exchange Theatre, Manchester); *Decades – Stories from the City*, *Europe*, *Around the World in Eighty Days*, *Be My Baby*, *Untold Stories* (Leeds Playhouse); *The Last Testament of Lillian Bilocca* (Hull UK City of Culture 2017); *Here's What She Said To Me*, *Tribes*, *The Effect* (Sheffield Theatres); *The Rise and Fall of Little Voice*, *Summer Holiday*, *The Big Corner*, *East is East*, *Jane Eyre*, *Winter Hill*, *The Tenant of Wildfell Hall*, *To Kill a Mockingbird*, *The Family Way*, *Private Lives*, *Duet for One*, *Separation*, *Robin Hood*, *Can't Pay? Won't Pay!* (Bolton Octagon Theatre); *Dr Blighty* (Nutkhut, 14-18 NOW, Brighton); *A Raisin in the Sun* (Eclipse/Sheffield Theatree/Belgrade Theatre/ UK tour); *The Massive Tragedy of Madame Bovary* (Liverpool Everyman & Playhouse, Peepolykus, Nuffield Theatre, Bristol Old Vic, Northampton Royal & Derngate, and UK tour); *Anon* (Welsh National Opera); *The Maw Broon Monologues* (Tron Theatre, Glasgow); *Faith Healer*, *North & South*, *Before the Party* (Pitlochry Festival Theatre); *The Masque of Anarchy* (Manchester International Festival); *Fireface* (Young Vic Theatre); *Manchester Sound: The Massacre*, *Manchester Lines* (Manchester Library Theatre); *Epstein* (Epstein Theatre, Liverpool/West End); *I Know Where the Dead are Buried* (24:7 Theatre Festival, Manchester); *Dark Side of the Building* (Unity Theatre, Liverpool); *Innovasion – Liverpool Biennial* (Hope Street Ltd.); *Four Corners* (Bluecoat Arts Centre, Liverpool); *Wish You Were Here* (Liverpool Everyman). Awards include: Best Design, Theatre Awards UK 2012, for *Manchester Lines*; Best Studio Production, Manchester Theatre Awards 2013, *Black Roses*; JMK Award 2012, Design for *Fireface.*

Alexandra Faye Braithwaite (Sound Designer)

Theatre credits include: *Wuthering Heights*, *Light Falls* (Royal Exchange Theatre); *Groan Ups* (Vaudeville Theatre); *Neville's Island* (Queen's Theatre Hornchurch); *The Audience*, *Juicy & Delicious* (Nuffield Theatre); *The Remains of Maisie Duggan* (Abbey Theatre); *Toast* (The Other Palace/Lowry Theatre/ Traverse Theatre); *Hamlet*, *Talking Heads*, *Rudolph* (Leeds Playhouse); *Things of Dry Hours* (Young Vic); *Cougar*, *Dealing With Clair*, *The Rolling Stone* (Orange Tree Theatre); *Romeo and Juliet* (China Plate); *Acceptance* (Hampstead Downstairs); *Chicken Soup* (Sheffield Crucible Studio); *Dublin Carol* (Sherman Theatre); *Kanye the First* (Hightide Festival); *Room* (Theatre Royal Stratford East/Abbey Theatre); *If I Was Queen* (Almeida); *The Tempest* (Royal & Derngate); *Diary of a Madman* (Gate Theatre/ Traverse Theatre); *A Christmas Carol* (Theatre Clwyd); *Simon Slack* (Soho Theatre); *Happy To Help* (Park Theatre); *The Future* (Yard Theatre); *My Beautiful Black Dog* (Southbank Centre); *Hamlet is Dead*, *No Gravity* (Arcola Theatre); *Remote* (Theatre Royal Plymouth); *Lonely Soldiers* (Arts Theatre); *Grumpy Old Women III* (UK tour).

Mark Distin Webster (Lighting Designer)

Mark has worked as a freelance lighting designer, programmer and technician as well as holding lighting technician posts at Contact Theatre and the RSC. He is currently a Lighting Lead at the Royal Exchange Theatre. Selected lighting design credits include: *I Hear Voices*, *Hatch* (Contact); *Nothing*, *Mixtape* (Royal Exchange Young Company); *Spinning Wheel* (Unfinished Business); *0.008*, *Song of Songs* (Weeding Cane); *Mr Sole Abode* (Madrugada); *Ghost Boy* (20 Stories High); *A Night on the Tiles* (Pen-Ultimate); *Late Night Love*, *Get A Round* (Eggs Collective); *Prelude to a Number* (Geddes Loom).

Yandass Ndlovu (Movement Director)

Founder of I M Pact Collective. Current Manchester International Festival Creative Fellow. First Class BA (Hons) Dance and Performance at the Arden School of Theatre (2019). Acting credits include: *Jubilee* (Lyric Hammersmith); *Macbeth*,

Our Town, *Nothing* (Royal Exchange Theatre, Manchester); *Birth*:
Orchid & Syria (World Health Organisation, Geneva); *Negging*
(Bristol Old Vic); *Dead Certain* (Hopemill Theatre).
Dance credits include: *Alphabus* (Manchester International
festival); *FlexN Manchester* (Old Granada Studios); *Flexn Young
Identity* (Contact Theatre); *Boy Blue Elevate* (HOME); *Festival
Number 6* (Portmeirion); *In Extremis* (Waterside Theatre).
Short Film and television credits include: *Icaria* (Nowness and
MIF); *Let's Go* supported by The Lowry, HOME, The Portico
Library, Contact, Opera House, Manchester, International
Anthony Burgess Foundation, Manchester Museum, Royal
Exchange Theatre; *Yandass.mov* (Random Acts, Channel 4);
The X Factor (ITV); *Run Boy Run* (Channel 4, Random Acts);
Freestyle (BFI); *All I Want For Christmas* (Royal Exchange Theatre
x I M Pact). Directing and Choreographing credits include:
Cryptomnesia (Future Ventures & ACE); *[M]others* (Co:lab – Royal
Exchange Theatre); *See Me After* – PUSH (HOME); *Fortitude*
(Short Film); *Yandass.mov* & *Run Boy Run* (Channel 4, Random
Acts); *Through The Eye* – Rachel Chinouriri. Assisting credits
include: *Breathe 2* (Manchester International Festival), *Space
Between Us* (Royal Exchange Theatre).

Hannah Sands (Associate Director)

Directing credits include: *Red Brick*, *Render* (Royal Exchange
Theatre); *Dick Whittington* (Leicester Square Theatre); *Obsession*
(Stockwell Playhouse/Katzpace Studio); *No Matter Where I
Go* (Arcola Theatre); *Aladdin* (Arts Theatre); *Human Animals*
(theSpace Edinburgh Fringe). Associate directing credits
include: *Connect Fest* (Royal Exchange Theatre). Assistant
directing credits include: *Wuthering Heights*, *Gypsy*, *Macbeth*
(Royal Exchange Theatre); *After the Ball* (The Gatehouse
Upstairs); *Dear Brutus* (Southwark Playhouse).

Manchester's Royal Exchange Theatre Company transforms the way people see theatre, each other and the world around them. Our historic building, once the world's biggest cotton exchange, was taken over by artists in 1976. Today it is an award-winning cultural charity that produces new theatre in-the-round, in communities, on the road and online.

Exchange remains at the heart of everything we make and do. Now our currency is brand new drama and reinvigorated classics, the boldest artists and a company of highly skilled makers – all brought together in a shared imaginative endeavour to trade ideas and experiences with the people of Greater Manchester (and beyond).

The Exchange's unique auditorium is powerfully democratic, a space where audiences and performers meet as equals, entering and exiting through the same doors. It is the inspiration for all we do; inviting everyone to understand the past, engage in today's big questions, collectively imagine a better future and lose themselves in the moment of a great night out.

The Royal Exchange was named Regional Theatre of the Year in 2016 and School of the Year at The Stage Awards 2018. Our work, developed with an incredible array of artists and theatre makers, includes *Hamlet* with Maxine Peake (for stage and film), *The Skriker* (with the Manchester International Festival), *King Lear* (co- produced with Talawa Theatre Company, filmed for BBC iPlayer and BBC Four), *The House of Bernarda Alba* (a co-production with Graeae), *Our Town* (directed by Sarah Frankcom), *Light Falls* (a world-premiere from Simon

Stephens directed by Sarah Frankcom with original music by Jarvis Cocker), *Wuthering Heights* (directed by Co-Artistic Director Bryony Shanahan), *Rockets and Blue Lights* (by award-winning writer Winsome Pinnock and directed by Miranda Cromwell), *The Mountaintop* (Digital Streaming directed by Roy Alexander Weise), *All I Want For Christmas* (digital commission for December 2020) and *Oh Woman!* (digital commissions for International Women's Day 2021).

For the Royal Exchange Theatre

Connecting Team
Andy Barry
Carys Williams
Claire Brown
Claire Will
Duncan Butcher
Inga Hirst
Isah-Levi Roach
Liam Steers
Lorraine Jubb
Martha Tomlinson
Morayo Sodipo
Neil Eskins
Paula Rabbitt
Philippa Crossman
Roy Alexander Weise
Scarlett Spiro-Beazley

Facilitating Team
Amelia Bayliss
Amy Drake
Brian Adgey
David Mitchell
Helen Brown
Jasper Samuels
Karen Haskey
Michelle Hickman
Mike Seal
Rachel Davies
Roma Melnyk
Serena Choudhary
Sharon Lever

Sheralee Lockhart
Simon Inkpen
Steve Freeman
Vicky Wormald
Yvonne Cox

Making Team
Bryony Shanahan
Carl Heston
Chloe Smith
Halima Arteh
Jo Shepstone
Justina Aina
Katie Vine
Louis Fryman
Mark Distin Webster
Matt Lever
Matthew Sims
Richard Delight
Sam Leahy
Sorcha Steele
Suzanne Bell
Tracy Dunk
Travis Hiner

Donors and Supporters

Rebel

Rebel Productions was formed to question why 'we've always done it like this' and to offer a fresh and exciting alternative to theatre producing and arts management. Taking ownership that caring is a strength, not a weakness, and to create and enable excellent work with formidable talent.

Rebel is led by Producer Peter J Holland in order to develop and curate projects outside of his work as producer of world-renowned theatre company Frantic Assembly. With over ten years of producing experience working for organisations such as The Birmingham Stage Company and London's Lyric Hammersmith, Rebel Productions enables Peter to bring together his knowledge and passion in producing high-quality work for national and international audiences under his own producing organisation. Rebel are committed to creating new work with a clear message that promotes equality and diversity, showcasing stories for all. Notably in 2020 Rebel produced the 'Passing Out Podcast' with presenter James Robert Moore detailing stories from LGBTQ+ service people in the British Army and was selected as 'podcast of the week' by Spotify in February. Rebel are excited to be collaborating on a new project with Black Skull Creative to be announced in Autumn 2021.

Rebel are delighted to have co-commissioned this world premiere and debut play by Lauryn Redding, *Bloody Elle – A Gig Musical*, with the Royal Exchange Theatre, Manchester. Having co-produced with the Royal Exchange on many other professional ventures it is extraordinary to be back in Manchester as Rebel celebrating the return of live theatre with exciting queer stories at the heart of the main stage.

Rebel are thrilled to support Lauryn Redding in penning her first play and joining the Royal Exchange Theatre to reopen post the global pandemic.

Little ideas in lockdown really did become an almighty wave.

www.peterjholland.com/rebel

www.bloodyelle.com

Social Media

Twitter: @RebelProds / @PeterJHolland

Instagram: @RebelProdPics

BLOODY ELLE
A Gig Musical

Lauryn Redding

For all the Elles.
And all the Eves…

Note on the Text

Bold text	Other people
Centered text	Lyrics/songs
Italics	Stage directions
–	A bounce of thought/A beat
…	A strain of thought/A beat
.	A considered moment/A beat
…/	No time to think or talk

ACT ONE

Pre-show music floods the auditorium.
The stage looks more like a gig than a play.

There are mics and mic stands,
an electric guitar
and an electro/acoustic guitar.
Loop pedals and guitar pedals.
The wires and the workings of the music aren't hidden.
They are laid bare for all to see.

The music is created live on stage and
all characters are voiced
by the actor.

The lights go down.
Anticipation.
ELLE *enters with a bottle of beer.*
She takes a swig.

She picks up her guitar
and begins.

UNPROLOGUE

Guitar loops are layered up.

Most shows start with a prologue,
Which I've always found quite odd.
Why tell the whole story? Wrap it up in a bow?
Like a giant fucking spoiler just to ruin your whole show?

So I won't start with a prologue.
As I said, I think they're quite odd.
Instead I'll just say, I hope you enjoy

It's not your average love story about a girl and a boy.
Loop builds vocally with beat boxing and harmonies.

It starts with a girl called Elle,
Yeah, she's not your average leading lady as well.
She has a heart the size of a moon,
She's been far from brought up with a silver spoon
In her gob.
She talks only the truth,
For her age she was long in the tooth.

–

Life was tough, she was tougher.
When life got rough, she got rougher.
Music builds.

Her head was in the clouds like hot air balloons,
Her heart was a full moon.
She knew the words
but she couldn't find the tune.

I'll stop, coz this sorta sounds like a prologue,
As I said, I think they're quite odd.
Instead I'll just say,
enjoy the play.
And oh
Music cuts out.

I'm Elle by the way.

Now then you lot.

How you doing?

You alright?

She encourages the audience to respond.

Thanks for coming.

It's a bit of punt coming to the theatre innit?

Bit risky.

Could be shit.

Could wish you hadn't bothered.

Coulda stayed in binge-watching *Homeland* on Netflix – Which is fucking brilliant by the way, if you haven't seen it! Goes down hill in the end tho, so wouldn't bother with about season three onwards. Clare Danes is (*Makes an 'amazing' gesture*.) in that! Although, I think she was at her best in Baz Luhrmann's *Romeo + Juliet*, but hey that's just me.

–

So, cheers – thanks for coming.

She raises her glass to the audience.

Most people I know only go to the theatre if they win tickets int paper or it's got Ben from A1 in it or something.

So, ta, really appreciate it.

–

I'm going to tell you all a story.

My story.

I'm gonna sing some songs, make some music and patch my way thru.

Amber's (*Or who ever is on the desk*.) on the desk making some magic too. Hi Amber!

See – music is my way of expressing – the lid comes off, no compressing.

We all feel it.

Them hairs – stand up – tingle.

We breathe it – arms open at a festival.

We mingle like the notes that intertwine and hit our ears.

Like the memories that flood back when you hear a song you haven't heard in years.

Some sit in an opera – clapping.

Some mosh pit – nose bleeds – guitar strings snapping.

Rapping.

Some bloke busking, commuters' feet tapping.

–

It's for people like me. That sound like me, look like me, feel what I feel – and for everyone else too.

So basically – if you're in here, it's for you!

–

Right – If you're sitting comfortably, I'll begin.

I hope you've got a pint or a gin in. Chin chin!

Let's rewind – back in time – to the summer of 2009.

We feel it is about to begin.

Oh.

One more thing.

I'm a potty mouth – I swear a lot.

Soz about that – it just falls out!

MAM. Gob shiiite…

That's me mam.

MAM. If you don't get your arse down here now, I'm chucking this casserole ont A64…

We live on floor ten.

Ten's the best floor –

Like – ten outta ten.

Like – Acting like you're 'ten men'.

Like – ten for the 'win'.

If you look down from up here, you feel like Simba or Mufasa, looking out over the city like you own it.

We don't.

Obviously.

Own it.

But we feel like we do.

It's in our bones, this place.

In our blood.

When you live here it's like you're instigated into some mad club –

Where everyone knows your shit and owns your shit.

Your-mess-is-mine mentality.

MAM. There's starving kids out there, don't you know?

Like one huge curtain-twitching family.

A vertical village.

All stacked on top of each other. Bringing sugar, milk and any other shit you run out of.

Remember once, Big Sally on floor twelve busted both of her knees. She couldn't walk for months. Everyone chipped in. Doing her big shop, getting her meds. Once the Duffield lads, there's six of em, they live on the sixth floor, carried Big Sally – all the way downstairs – FROM THE TWELFTH FLOOR, just coz she couldn't remember what grass felt like.

Yeah.

.

When people drive past here, I swear they drive faster.

They don't like looking at it.

Us.

The high-rise that blinds their eyes.

But it's ours.

Legit.

Feels like we own it.

–

I'm proud to be from Cloudrise.

That's what me dad called it.

–

I sit – in my room – ten floors closer to the clouds and the moon.

Play guitar. Lose hours. Sing songs. Watch the sky go all mad colours. Pinks, yellows and shades of orange that look like you can taste em.

I watch the sunrise, if I'm up,
the sunset almost daily.

The moon sits hovering in the blue skies hazy – Then glows hard at night, like it's drunk from its daydream.

–

From Cloudrise you can see the whole city.

Look.

There's the city centre in the middle just chilling – with roads spinning around it – with cars trickling.

There's other high-rises scattered nearby.

A park. Some footy fields, my old school and a sign,

'THE HOME OF THE TUBULAR BANDAGE'

True story.

We invented it.

Proud of it.

MAM. Seriously, this scran is off int bin!

If you squint real hard, you've got the posh bit out west.

Big houses. Bobbing int hills.

MAM. Ten, nine

Spreading out over east, you've got the 'normal' houses –

Your two-up two-down jobbys.

Showing off, all owned and that.

MAM. Eight, seven

And I think…

You lot don't get this.

You can't see this.

MAM. Six, five

We float in the clouds.

They look down on us,

MAM. Four, three

but really we are looking down on them.

MAM. DANIELLE!!!

Me mam's the only person that calls me Danielle.

I fucking hate it.

Everyone else calls me Elle.

My brother, 'Shitbrick'– he calls me b-Elle end.

It's actually quite funny, annoyingly, but I'd never tell him that.

MAM. You coming or what?

ELLE. Alright – I'm coming I'm coming…

MAM. Well – you're cutting it fine…

ELLE. Calm your farm Mam – I've plenty time! – Whoa – UGH You've fucking double-microwaved this!

Surprise casserole. Fuck knows what the surprise is – but I've got third-degree burns from a potato and my eyeballs are popping out me eyelids.

She's no Delia, my mam, but she does her best.

You know them No 1 Mam mugs…? Yeah? That's her.

ELLE. Right-am-off-bye…

MAM. Oi, kiss?

She taps her cheek. You know, how mams do?

A kiss – A peck.

Ont bike.

Bezz it to work.

I work at one of the finest establishments round here.

The crème de la crème.

It's where all the cool kids work.

All of them.

I work –

Full time at –

'Chips and Dips'.

Yeah –

Granted.

It's no one's first choice. But it suits me fine.

I didn't get many qualifications like. I am proper clever tho, I just wasn't in school much.

So, I got a job at Chips and Dips part-time. Liked it, went full-time. And now I spend most my time there. Been here three year now.

It's pretty good craic, Chips and Dips,

and you get free chips and dips too.

So.

–

It's not a chippy.

Although we do do chips.

It's more like… You know Subway? Yeah? Well, like that but with crisps, nachos and shit. We also do butties and barms. Basically carbs.

If it's beige, we sell it.

BARRY (*thick Welsh accent*). **Ahhh I see, she's decided to turn up has she…**

Oh, that's my boss. Big Barry. He's Welsh. In case you hadn't realised.

BARRY. It always shocks me Danielle. For such an excellent worker, your time management is quite appalling.

ELLE. Sorry Baz, it won't happ–

BARRY. You gotta keep that head out the clouds girl, and keep it on the main prize… chips and dips.

ELLE. Sorry Baz, it won't happ–

BARRY. Good. Now… follow me. I have a task for you today young Dani. We have a new-bie, a fresh-ie, a… Somebody who's not worked here before-ie. She needs showing the ropes. And the chips and dips.

This is Evelyn.

–

Posh hair.

Top knot.

New uniform.

Jammy bastard.

Fresh kicks.

New Air Maxes.

She's got a freckle on her chin.

EVE. Hi. Erm… It is Evelyn. But, please – just call me… Eve.

Sorry – I should introduce you to everyone else really shouldn't I?! How rude.

So – We've got Big Barry,

BARRY. Alright.

…you've met him.

Then there's Eddie.

EDDIE. Wheeeey, iya babes!!

Wide as he is tall. He's harmless, totally useless and always has a story to tell. Whether it's true or not, that's up to you!

EDDIE. You'll never believe it! Last night I was at 'Spoons and I choked on a new potato. No joke. So – mid-choke – I thought 'fuck it'– did a handstand in the middle of the bar and coughed it out. I've still got it in me pocket. Dya wanna see?!

Then there's arr Jack.

JACK (*nods*). Now then.

Jack is a man of few words. But his words are usually excellent.

He's a beanpole. Still rocking the curtains and probably the nicest guy I know.

Then there's Amy.

AMY. Ohmygod – never guess what…!

She's pot wash mainly coz when she's out front she talks too much and does everyone's head in.

She's dead nice, don't get me wrong! But I wouldn't trust her as far as I could throw her – You know the ones?

Then there's 'twat'– I mean, Aaron.

AARON (*sings Johnny Cash 'Ring of Fire' like he's on a Stag do*). **Oi oi you massive dickheads. Don't worry, I've arrived!**

Aaron is 'one of The Lads'. A different girl every night and always talking about how big his knob is. Although he sent a dick pic to Amy once…

AMY.…and it looked like it'd been slammed in a car door.

So…

Aaron attempts to chat up a girl on the front row.

AARON. Hiya sweetheart. I've lost my phone number, can I have yours?

Sorry about him.

He's a good-looking lad to be fair. Just a shame he's a dick.

He tried it on with me a few times when I first started.

I told him I'd rather shit in my hands and clap.

And then there's me. Elle. Holding the fort, or so I'd like to think.

We're like the Bash Street Kids, us. A dysfunctional family. Like a mad melting pot of humans, but it works actually.

–

So, Eve's arrival really messed up the chips.

Mixed the guac with the salsa.

Put the sour-cream spoon in with the baba ganoush.

Everyone was on shift that day and everyone was acting weird!

–

BARRY. Bore da, pawb – ladies and gentlemen – boys and girls. Welcome to the staff briefing.

We have a staff briefing at the start of every shift – Just to divvy up the jobs and shit. Poor Bazza normally can't get a word in edgeways and then we all go off and do what we want anyways. So no point really. We form a circle int kitchen, well more of a squished square to be fair –

But today – With Eve on the scene.

Silence.

Never seen a more perfect circle.

Best behaviours all round.

Everyone looking at Eve when they can get away with a glimpse. She looks so different to any of us I think. Dunno what it is.

BARRY. May I introduce our new recruit – Evelyn! Welcome to the family.

She tries to talk, but she's got phlegm stuck in her throat –

EVE (*coughs*)**....Oh... Hello. Please...** (*Coughs*.) **just call me Eve.**

Jobs divvyed.

Soliders salute.

Scatter.

It's just me and Eve, behind the front counter.

–

She's about my height.

Maybe taller.

About my age too I reckon.

Red hair.

Her ears are well little.

She's got bracelets with charms on, and rings on her fingers.

ELLE. You'll have to take them off...

EVE. Pardon, sorry what?

ELLE. Them rings and that. You'll have to take em off.

EVE. Oh, okay, erm... sorry! Erm... right, off? Yes.

She's fumbling, taking them off. I was gonna offer to help for a second, but that'd be weird wouldn't it?

Yeah.

Her hands look well soft – Never worked a day in her life I reckon. Look at my hands in comparison. Rough – chipped.

–

I spoon the dips for a bit – y' know? Keep em fresh.

ELLE. So, I haven't seen you round here before, what brings you here then? Is it your love for an assorted range of chips and dip-idge?

She looks at me.

Eyeballs wide.

She has a look in her eyes, right.

Really innocent.

I've not really seen it before.

Apart from in dogs.

Or babies.

It's like she's really listening to me. Looking into my soul a bit. It's a bit much.

EVE. Oh no, I'm new. New round here. Erm, from London. My dad got a new job up here so, yes, we've come 'to the north!'

ELLE. From London. Mint. Never been. Any good?

**EVE. Ooh London? London's London…! But… erm… I
start university in September, so just up here for a short
while really, until I go.**

ELLE. University. Wow. Big shit that. What you studying… in?

**EVE. Oh boring stuff really. Medicine? Erm… I come from
a family of doctors you see. So, just following suit. I'd
love to go travelling but Daddy says 'Travelling can wait!'
But, I'm excited for university… How about you? What
do you study?**

I've never met anyone like this in my life.

Medicine? Travelling?

A family of doctors?

DADDY?!

ELLE. Me? Nah – I'm not studying owt me. Just work here.
Full time.

I play music and stuff, gig a bit.

But mainly just – making sure the right chip goes with the
right dip.

It's like an alien's been chucked an apron and plonked on the
front counter with me. How's she ended up working here?!

She keeps looking at me.

Staring.

It's freaking me out if I'm honest.

Don't posh people blink?!

**EVE. Wow! That's amazing… Music…?! What kind?
Erm… What do you play?**

She's got really green eyes.

Same colour as the guacamole actually.

ELLE. Guitar... And sing a bit.

She freckle on her chin looks like a bit of chocolate.

I think it is chocolate?

EVE. I get really envious when I meet people who can play instruments. I always wish I'd stuck at it, you know, as a child. But I was... erm... forced to play clarinet at school, and clarinet was never cool was it! It looks like you're carrying a mini-briefcase! Hah.

ELLE. Clarinet? Nah, they're mint. There's a mad song called – Ahhhh what is it – Errrr, 'Rhapsody in Blue'. The clazza on that is proper good. I used to listen to it on my dad's vinyl.

EVE. Vinyl? Wow. That's cool... does he have a large collection?

ELLE. Oh he did. He's dead now.

EVE. Gosh I'm so sorry...

ELLE. Nah it's okay –

EVE. No I – I always put my big old feet in it. I'm so sorry –

ELLE. It's fine – don't apologise ...

EVE. No... I'm so so so sorry.

ELLE. It's fine mate. You didn't kill him.

EVE. No I didn't...

–

She spoons the dips for a bit, you know? Keep em fresh.

But she hasn't quite got the knack of it yet.

–

It's really awkward. Figure I better break the ice...

I do the only thing I know how –

I whack out my imaginary clarinet.

ELLE *sings the clarinet line from 'Rhapsody in Blue'.*

She's laughing.

I am pretty funny to be fair.

ELLE (*clarinet continues*).

She's whacked out her imaginary clarinet too!

EVE/ELLE *play together,* EVE *has a soprano/operatic version.*

EVE. I'd love to see you… Come to one of your – concerts – gigs erm…

Annnnnd. (*Sniffs.*) Can you smell that?

She encourages the audience to sniff.

Sniff hard and you might just catch it.

Got it?

Yep.

That is the waft of desperation. Or Bugo Hoss.

Enter Twat –

AARON. Oi oi ladies! How you doing? Now then Eve – Eva Diva – do you believe in love at first sight? Or should I walk in again?

She giggles like a schoolgirl.

Why do lasses do that?

–

The next eight hours consist of 'trying to impress Eve', or as I like to call it – 'dick swinging.'

AARON. Let me guess yeah? Your middle name is Gillette right? Coz you're the best a man can get.

Even Big Barry's giving it a go.

BARRY. Ahhh, I see, well – sometimes, Eve you just gotta roll your sleeves up and eat the custard.

Amy's pure fuming.

AMY. Errmmmm ohmygod I'm not being snide or owt, Eve seems dead nice. But it's like she's royalty or something. Do you think it's her posh hair?

Jack's keeping out the way, busy clearing trays.

JACK. That's gonna happen. Them two. I give it three days.

He's a man of few words, arr Jack, but he's rarely wrong.

–

Shift done.

Bezz it home.

Level out.

Ten floors closer to the clouds.

THE SAME

It's all the same,

Every day.

It's all the same,

Round our way.

So, why change,

When it works this way?

Why change?

I like it the same.

The following week ticks by pretty nicely.

So to speak.

Standard week.

Although there's a weird change in the air and I really don't know what it was.

–

Work's fine.

I leave the 'dick swingers' to it.

AARON. Eve – right – if you were a chicken – yeah? You'd be im-peck-able.

She's still giggling. Enjoying the attention.

AARON. What?! You've never been Vodka Revs? You've never lived babe. I'll take you. They do five Jägers for a tenner, but my mate knows the guy who invented Jägerbombs – so I get a deal…

I leave my imaginary clarinet in my locker.

I'm not rude to her or owt – Still chat to her, but the boys are like flies round shit.

She gets the hang of work pretty quickly tho. She smashes the till system – which is impressive in itself because there's seventeen different types of chip, forty-three different assortments of dips available, then you've got your drinks and your sundries, that's before you've even dealt with butties, barms and meal deals. So you need to go to uni for that alone, to be honest!

She's getting on with everyone.

Customers,

staff,

Aaron.

Specially Aaron.

Arr Jack were right about that one!

JACK. Told you so…

Oh – and I realise that freckle on her chin was a bit of chocolate.

It's gone now.

It's all the same,
Every day.
It's all the same,
Round our way.

No games,
No win or lose – Just the same?
Why change?
No danger this way..

AARON. Oi oi! Listen up you bunch of pricks…

Aaron's jumped on top of a standing freezer, banging a pan with a ladle, just in case the whole fucking world couldn't already hear him.

AARON. Tomorrow night, it's the 'Annual Chips and Dips Summer Sesh'! Now I know you've all been dying to know what I've been planning this year… well, we are going… to… drum roll please dickheads…!?

The audience are encouraged to join in tapping on their knees or table.

AARON.…Megabowl, you bastards! And then Vodka Revs, obvs! So, as total hero and overall captain of fucking banter. This year is gonna be Meggaaa… bowl!

AMY. Errr Aaron, dickhead. What's the theme? The fancy-dress theme?!

AARON. Oh yeah, shit… fancy-dress theme is – 'who or what you wanted to be when you were little!' I'm going dressed as a fucking legend.

The 'Annual Chips and Dips Summer Sesh' is always a proper laugh. It's nice to see old staff, people really go for the fancy dress and I'm not bothered about the bowling but I'm really good at them machines where you have to stack the blocks on top of each other. Won a sandwich toaster once.

BARRY. Many thanks Aaron for organising. Tomorrow, we will shut up shop ten minutes early so we can get our gladrags on. I will be going dressed as a Chippendale. Because it was always my dream.

As that little bit of sick that came into my mouth went back down...

EVE. Elle? Is this a thing then? Erm... the summer sesh? Gosh. Shit.

I hadn't heard her swear before.

EVE. Gosh – I'm already nervous...

Weird, coz even tho she said she was nervous. She has this confidence. Confidence in a way I'd not seen in someone before.

Quietly confident.

Normally if you're confident round our way, you're really loud – Shouty and probably have a shit car that looks like a shopping trolley and sounds like a lawnmower.

EVE....And fancy dress! Gosh! I've only got one fancy-dress outfit I can think of and I don't think it quite fits the brief!

I didn't want her to be nervous.

I don't know why?

ELLE. Ahh. Listen – Don't worry. It's no biggie. Just wear whatever!

EVE. No biggie – wear whatever... okay.

ELLE. Just – maybe – don't come as a clarinet player...

Here I am.

Here we are.

Megabowl!

–

See, I thought it was a nationwide thing, me, until I spoke to
someone recently and they'd never heard of it! If you know
it, you'll get my drift. If you don't. Welcome! Megabowl is
iconic. And if you had a Megabowl birthday party, well...
You were the tits.

It's a bowling place –

With a Wimpy inside!

Every arcade game under the sun.

The nostalgic waft of burgers, popcorn and shoe-freshening
spray.

–

I'm dressed as a long-distance lorry driver.

Legit.

When I was a kid I was borderline OBSESSED with Eddie
Stobarts.

Trucker hat with a silhouette of a naked girl on it, one of
my dad's old flannel shirts, jeans and a wifebeater vest. Oh
and one arm painted pink from hanging out the window and
getting sunburnt.

–

Everyone's starting to rock up.

ELLE. Alrright Charlie!

...Charlie's ace. She left about six months ago.

She's working in Butlin's now as a Redcoat. She's come
dressed in a red coat actually. Bit lazy that? Or maybe she's
come straight from work.

Tash's come as a slutty nurse... Any opportunity to get her
tits out.

Amy –

Jesus wept – She's come as Marge Simpson.

Painted herself fully yellow!

Barry – a vicar!? Bit of a curve ball – He's obviously chickened out of the Chippendale outfit. We'll all be glad of that.

Paige – cheerleader.

Greeny – tree surgeon.

And then, Eve…

–

Now you won't believe it right –

But she comes in…

She comes in dressed as a whoopee cushion.

A fucking whoopee cushion.

This new girl.

Brazen.

Zero fucks.

I didn't think she had it in her.

–

She comes running over to me – Well, waddling really.

EVE. Oh thank god you're here Elle… I had this horrible feeling on the way that I was going to be the only one and it was all a joke and now there's tons of people I don't know and I'm a bloody whoopee cushion. Shit.

She's funny when she swears.

EVE. I should have come as doctor really shouldn't I? But I thought… erm… this might have more suckerpunch… You know? Gosh. I didn't quite get the brief right did I? I knew I was slightly barmy for putting this on. But sod it. At least I'll go out with a…

ELLE....Bang?

EVE. Exactly – oh my gosh, Elle, you look… amazing! Nice
tan –

She puts her hand on my painted pink arm.

And that.

–

You know those moments in your life? Those moments you
didn't realise were a moment, until you look back and go
'ohhh that was a moment.'

Well this was one of those 'moment moments'.

–

She put her hand on my painted pink arm.

It was nice. Like ice. Like nice ice. Like when you're too hot
and you put a cold can of pop on your neck to cool down.

Them hairs – stand up – tingle.

Her hand. So soft. You know the rings and bracelets she took
off? Well, they're still gone – there's just tan lines now, like
memories of a past life… or summit.

–

A whoopee cushion and a long-distance lorry driver.

And her guacamole-green eyes –

That look into my soul a bit.

And the gap where the freckle used to be.

And that quiet confidence she has that escapes all gravity –
that shoots up thru the clouds – round the moon – and back
to me –

and her.

Here.

STOP THE WORLD

Stop the world, I wanna get off.

This feeling has shook my heart and almost blown my head off.

Please stop – I wanna get off,

I was fine until this moment, now the floor's opened up.

Please stop.

I'm buzzing. My head's gone hot – fuzzy.

Suddenly the foyer is full. Busy. A vet, a mechanic, a footballer and..

Please

Stop, before it's too late,

Before this feeling overrides me and I can't think straight.

Is it hot in here or is that just me...?

I think I want to kiss her what the fuck is happening?

She stands with those hands,

I watch her every day.

I haven't known what I've been feeling,

but it hasn't gone away...

She came in on Wednesday in a T-shirt that was grey...

I wanted her to wear it every day.

Forever...

I don't know why but,

Whatever.

Please Please

stop,

I wanna get off.

AARON. Oi oi you set of knobheads! The man of the hour has arrived.

Aaron's literally come dressed as himself.

No costume.

Just 'legend' written on his forehead.

Prick.

He's coming straight over to us, I already want him to fuck off.

I look down. Her hand's gone.

AARON. A whoopee cushion! Babe. Eve. What did you wanna be when you were little?! A fart?! What the actual fuck man?! Still best-looking bird in here by far tho...

He shoots me a look.

That's for all the times I told him I'd rather shit in my hands and clap.

He grabs Eve by her hand, that hand and drags her towards the bar.

I really hate him right now. Like, an amount of hate that makes my insides hurt a bit.

She's looking at me.

It's like she's trying to say something and I don't know what.

–

Aaron props up the bar.

Lording it up.

Like a shepherd with all his sheep flocking up.

Eve's still looking at me.

Suddenly – he pulls the rubber toggy thing off her head.

Her red hair falls down, it's quite long actually.

And then –

he kisses her.

Loop stops.

–

–

–

Loop starts.

EDDIE. Wheeeey 'iya babes! You look great! Nice cossie! Hey – check me out – g'day mateeee!

Eddie's stuck tampons to a cowboy hat to get the 'Steve Irwin Aussie look'.

EDDIE. I'm a zookeeper babe. I met Steve Irwin at Chester Zoo once and he said I had a gift.

Arr Jack –

JACK. Now then… (*Elvis impression.*)

Elvis. And he's eating a Wimpy. Attention to detail, on point.

EDDIE. Babes, you're wiv us on lane four. Mad Wendy's here! She's come as a marine biologist and brought a real goldfish in a bag!!

…

Elle.

…

Elle. You okay babes?

…

ELLE. Yeah sorry mate… fucking hell.

EDDIE. Let's get some Jägers in, that'll sort you out. Aaron's at the bar now – he gets a deal coz he knows the guy who invented them! Also, between you and me, I reckon he's getting his end away tonight with the newbie.

Come on…

Wild. Fucking. Horses would not take me to that bar right now.

ELLE. I'm alright Eddie mate. I'm just gonna… erm…

JACK.…Go for a smoke?

Jack hands me his cigs and a lighter.

He has this way about him, arr Jack.

ELLE. Yeah, a smoke. Cheers pal.

WHAT AM I FEELING?
I'm smoking, choking, not really knowing what is going on.
Been feeling reeling since the moment of our meeting.
What is going down? Why can't I keep this down?
Let it pass.
What am I feeling?

Just keep on breathing, let this nicotine fill my system,
I need a gin, a pint.
I need to get fucking steaming.
What has happened? Am I dreaming?
Something shot straight thru my veins
What am I feeling?

When he grabbed her hand, I couldn't understand.
But I had this feeling falling over me
Like quicksand.
When her red hair fell,
I fell as well –
And then he kissed her,
Fucking…

EVE....Elle? Hi. Oh – I thought we'd – erm – lost you. Ooh. A ciggie? Erm... may I... have a drag?

ELLE. Yeah course.

I don't think she smokes, she's doing that thing where she holds it weird and doesn't really take it back.

EVE (*stifling a cough*). **Apparently I'm on lane six, how about you?**

ELLE. Four.

She passes me the cig back.

Her fingers clench the filter tip – Tight, knuckles white.

Our fingers touch a bit.

EVE. Cool. Well... erm... I'll see you in there?

–

Then she walks – well, waddles back in.

–

She seems nervous?

Maybe that's the nicci rush.

Or maybe she felt it too.

WHAT AM I FEELING? Reprise
What just happened? Am I dreaming?
Let it pass...
What am I feeling?

Full musical release.

Guitar, vocals and sound builds.

Everything stops.

Monday.

Work.

Same shit, different day.

Or at least I wish it felt that way.

AMY. Errrr... Ohmygod you shoulda gone dressed as 'Where's Wally' babe, we were looking for you all night! You missed all the goss... neverguesswhat??

Amy's still a tinge of yellow. She looks like she's got jaundice.

EDDIE. You sneaky bugger! We lost ya! You missed me finally necking on with that barmaid from Revs – her dad owns Tesco, so I'm gonna be in the money.

He doesn't own Tesco. He works on the one down Leeman Road.

JACK. Now then. You alright?

I'm fine...? Why's everyone asking me how I am??

BARRY. Ahhhh... Danielle! Nearly sent out a search party for you Saturday. Sniffer dogs the lot! You okay?

AMY. Ohmygod, you okay?

EDDIE. Babes – you okay?

JACK. You alright?

If people keep asking me if I'm okay I'm gonna SLAM MY HEAD IN A LOCKER.

ELLE. I'm fine. I just... erm... I lost a... contact lens... So I called it in.

EDDIE. Didn't know you wore contact lenses?

I don't.

ELLE. I do.

Then – The moment came. The moment I'd been dreading – The moment I'd been waiting for – What'd been doing my head in –

Eve and Aaron walk in, together. Aaron with his arm draped over her, basking in his glory like he's carrying the FA fucking cup.

My stomach flips, hurts a bit.

AARON. Oi oi dickheads! Whey – here she is! Elle 'the fucking trucker'... where'd you fuck off to?

ELLE. Ahh, I just called it in mate. You've still got Sharpie on your head by the way...

AARON. Yeah, I know... Legend. Eh – you looked like a right dyke on Saturday. 'Delivery to sixty-nine muffdive drive!! Oi oi.'

–

They all laugh – So I laugh too.

–

Front counter.

Spoon the dips.

I feel sick.

Wipe the sides.

Right trays – in the right piles.

Spoon the dips.

Spoon the dips.

Spoon the...

The kitchen door swings open behind me.

Footsteps towards me.

Please don't be Eve.

Please don't be Eve.

Please don't be...

ELLE. Eve. Alright mate? Good night Saturday?

EVE. Yes. Fun. Bit mad. Don't think I want to drink again for a while! Especially Jägerbombs. Aaron knows the guy...

ELLE.…who invented them. Yeah I know.

I can't look at her.

She's doing that thing where she looks at me like no one else ever has.

EVE. Erm… Are you okay Elle? You just disappeared?

ELLE. Oh honestly I'm good mate. I think I had a dodgy Wimpy or something and once we got out out, I… erm.. I lost a contact lens, so I called it in. Also, Mad Wendy swallowed her goldfish, and it sent me west!

EVE. Yes. I saw that. You were trying to make her throw it up into a glass of water.

ELLE. Yeah. Poor bastard. Don't think anyone deserves to spend much time in Mad Wendy's insides! Even if they have got a four-second memory…

She's STILL looking at me in that way. I wish she'd just fuck off.

EVE. Listen Elle – erm… Are you busy this week? I wondered if you…? Do you — erm… Would you like to hang out?

What the fuck?

ELLE. Errr yeah? I've got a gig tomorrow night?

ELLE *is backstage,*
behind a curtain at Little John's Pub.

She is waiting to be called on stage.

The bar is busy.

A band can be heard playing on stage. They're giving it their all.

Here I am.

Here we are.

Little John's.

My local.

Played here a million times.

Well – not a million.

But a fair few like.

But this time…

Well,

Never.

In my life.

Have I been shitting myself.

This much.

I gig all the time. It's where I feel most safe. Here. Behind my guitar.

But tonight, well I dunno.

My mind's skipping – willing – wishing – thinking. Why did I even invite her?! I hope she doesn't turn up! Maybe she'll go to the wrong pub? Maybe she'll get lost? Maybe there'll be a tornado and this place will go up like Wizard of fucking Oz? I don't know.

Right now I wish I was in Cloudrise – safe up high, ten floors closer to the sky.

A final blast is heard from the band onstage – Who finish their song with enthusiasm.

JULIE. Let's hear it for Simon and the Shoelaces. Cheers lads. Oop, mind your step there Tim. Right – next up, back by popular demand. We've got arr local lass – Elle. Make some noise –

This part feels live.

Lights come up on the audience a bit.

She takes to the mic.

ELLE. Now then…

Nice to be back at Little John's. Thanks for having me Julie.

I'm gonna start off with a new song actually.

It's called 'Losing Control'.

LOSING CONTROL
What was that?
My heart just jumped inside my chest,
It feels like cardiac arrest.
And to be honest I don't know what to do next.

Coz I've found in the past, that thinking too much can be
a sin,
So I'm thinking less and just doing.
Just doing what my heart believes in.

Am I tripping? Coz my palms are all sweaty and I'm
shaking,
I catch myself daily daydreaming,
My head in the clouds and I'm flying

CHORUS
As time, goes by, it's like I'm high…

And there she is. That grey T-shirt. Red hair – down.

CHORUS
As time, goes by, it's like, I'm constantly high.
And my heart is beating,
and my head is dreaming,
and my feet are tapping,
and my hands are clapping,
and my back is arching,

and my toes are curling
and I might stop breathing. Am I losing control of it all...?
Am I losing control of it all?
I'm losing control...

The room is full – but for a second it's like it's just her
and me.

She's sat at the bar, well – stood actually. Clapping –
whooping –

She keeps whooping – It's making me laugh.

I smash thru the rest of my set.

–

**EVE. Oh my goodness. Honestly wow. Like. You're.
Amazing. Gosh. I. Okay. I really need to calm down – but
shit me.**

Sit at the bar. A pint. A gin. Ta Julie!

**Okay – I've got an admission to make... I, I erm... I've
never been to a gig before! This is my first ever gig. I
know, it's... weird... bit mad... erm... but yes! Wow, just,
wow, this, you, goodness, gosh, you have blown my mind!**

When she talks she has no filter and it explodes out of her
mouth like Skittles on them adverts.

**I mean – I've been to concerts and musicals. But never a
gig...**

ELLE. Musicals?! Eve you're mad you! Well, look – there's
loadsa shit I've never done, so! I'll take it as a compliment.
Being your first.

–

We chat.

For hours.

She's got a mam and a dad, two brothers and two sisters. She
grew up in Godalming? Which sounds made up to me.

She went to boarding school down there too. She used to sleep at her school?! How mad's that!

She's off to university in September. Oxford.

I think she's minted. I'd kinda guessed already from the posh hair, and her kicks and the way she talks about stuff I've never heard of. But she goes skiing and shit – and that's expensive int it?

ELLE. Ta Julie! Did you do archery and shit in PE at school? I always thought, maybe I'm a shit-hot archer, but I'll never know coz I've never tried.

She's got a jacuzzi in her house.

How the hell has she ended up working at Chips and Dips?

EVE. I wanted to get a job and meet some friends round here. Also my dad didn't like the idea of me working in a 'chippy'– So I did it to piss him off… And honestly? I really like chips!

I talk about my family.

Which never happens.

But I feel like I can.

Not that I'm ashamed or owt, but I'm quite private really.

I tell her how we lost Dad, and about Mam's depression.

About my brother 'Shitbrick', the apprentice joiner and arsehole.

Tell her about Cloudrise.

She tells me her favourite colour is blue coz when she were little, blue Smarties gave her a kick.

I tell her –

ELLE. Having a favourite colour's daft, coz all colours are amazing.

–

EVE. Okay, if you were a biscuit, what biscuit would you be?

ELLE..../

EVE. I'd be a pink wafer. Because you forget about them, but when you have one you wonder 'why are these not an essential part of my everyday life.' Go on. Your go, biscuit.

ELLE..../

EVE. No!? You haven't got one? Okay, well I've got yours – if you don't. You're a chocolate Hobnob...

ELLE..../

EVE. Because, well firstly they're everyone's favourites. They're reliable and never let you down. But also – also – from the exterior you're quite hard looking but once you're dipped into a cup of tea you're a big softie really.

Silence – a beat – a moment.

I realise how different we are.

In every – single – way.

But I've never felt more... at home.

EVE. Thanks Julie. Have you ever just thought fuck it... I'm going to do this music thing? Shit – Elle, you totally should! Do it! Be a recording artist – travel the world – play your music in bars and theatres and concert halls across the globe, and have merchandise – little badges and posters you can sign – people knowing the lyrics to your songs. Shit! You could do that! You're good enough...

She goes a little pink in the face when she's saying that.

ELLE. Ahhh – I dunno. I've never allowed myself to go there, in my head, if you know what I mean? I've never really thought 'bout venturing far from here to be honest. Sad that innit? Coz it's a bit shit really.

(*Pause.*) I've never been on a plane. I've never been to London. I've never done much out the ordinary to be honest...

Just looking at her makes me feel – invincible. Like, if the roof came off I could fly.

I've never wanted for owt, don't get me wrong! But I never really felt like I could do those things, those big things. Coz those things aren't for me – They don't happen to us. And if you never want em, then you're never disappointed. God that sounds depressing doesn't it? But... Yeah... I guess, now you mention it... You can be anything you want in the whole wide world really, can't you?

Silence – a beat – a moment.

ELLE. Same again please, Julie.

Just gonna go for a –

–

I sit.

In the cubicle.

Pants down.

Don't need a piss.

Need a minute.

I've never felt – How this feels – How I feel.

Ever.

Fuck. Shit.

Every movement, her fingers, her hands, her green eyes that dart and dance. I'm drawn to her, like flies to blue light. And it never ends well for them does it? Shite.

Her perfume, that smell – Wanna breathe her in and never breathe out.

Fucking hell.

Grey T-shirt, red hair.

Keep looking away coz I don't wanna stare

Fuck. Shit.

–

–

–

Am I...?

Am I?

Fuck. Shit.

Am I...?!

Am I all those awful things people say?!

Fuck. Shit.

Shit. Fuck.

–

ELLE. Hi –

I'm back.

We chat.

Sip arr sups.

The bar lights flash to hurry us up.

Time's sped up.

We're outside suddenly.

And there she is –

Stood in front of me.

I think we're both pissed.

There's something in my stomach and I think it's got wings...

Fuck. Shit.

I LIKE YOU
I like you,
There I said,
fuck shit,
I like you.
I dunno how it happened,
But I like you.
I don't know where it came from,
But I...
Need to stop saying I like you.

When I saw you,
I wondered who the fuck had brought you.
My stomach did this thing I didn't know it could do.
head got hot,
heart got fast,
hands got clammy too.
Coz I'm pacing,
waiting –
for you to start your shift,
All their faces, looking, knowing,
thinking I'm a disgrace
If they knew how I liked you,
The way that I like you...

So I pushed it down
now it's overflowing,
I don't even know where this conversation's going.

This is an admission
It's not really a decision.
I don't know the definition,
But at night I get these visions.

Of you and me,

holding hands,

we've been to bars,

drank all jars,

it's dark,

and there's stars,

passing cars playing Bruno Mars...

You should feel my heart.

Silence – a beat – a moment.

...she turns and walks away.

–

I need a smoke.

This is a joke.

My hands – my fingers can't find the flame.

I'm shaking like a shitting dog and regretting.

Every last breath – every last syllable – every fucking thought that passes thru my head...

Is pitiful.

Fuck my life.

Why'd I spout that shite?! Now she's gonna think I'm a... D –

Shut up.

What's wrong with me?

This isn't normal – This isn't me...

–

A hand.

On my arm.

A grip.

It was nice. Like ice. Like nice ice.

She's come back.

Her hand – soft – quietly confident – She pulls me down t'ginnel round the side of the bar.

It's dark.

Her guacamole greens in the moonlight almost stop my heart.

–

Eyes lock.

Then bang – like a jack in a box, she grabs me by my top. Her lips hit mine like a car-crash collision.

A kiss.

The world stops.

Her lips are well soft.

–

I pull her in for more.

Push against the brick – My hands up her back, they're cold but she likes it. I think.

Her thighs between mine.

Now I don't know what the fuck I'm doing.

But nothing has ever felt so normal in my ENTIRE life.

–

MUM. Gobshiiite! Tea's ont table in ten!

Back in Cloudrise, watching the blue skies. Being Simba, or Mufasa. Looking down. Looking up. Playing my guitar and not giving a fuuuuck!

Few days have passed since that night.

THE night.

I think the fear, and the happiness exploded together to create this nugget. This secret little nugget of amazing, beautiful, scary shit. And it sits here now.

She places nugget in her chest.

I lie in bed and I just replay it.

Over and over.

The way she grabbed me – her hand – her smell – her lips – her hips.

MUM. Danielle!! Nearly ready!

I bounce into the kitchen – Jump up ont side.

ELLE (*whistles*)….What?

MUM. What's up with you?

ELLE. Nowt?

MUM. You're being weird. Whistling?

ELLE. I'm just happy I guess? It's not illegal.

MUM. Right… D'ya want beans or hoops?

ELLE. Hoops, ta…

I stare at the chicken-shaped basket on the side, piled with eggs. And I wonder how Eve would like her eggs in a morning.

Scrambled –

She starts singing.

– boiled or fried. As long as I get my kiss…

MUM. Right, who is he?

ELLE. What?

MUM. Who is he? I'm not an idiot, Danielle. The boy. The lad. Who's got you smitten. Who is he?

–

ELLE. Steve.

MUM. Right…? Go on then, Steve? Which Steve? Oh not Steve Midgley from floor eight is it? I hope not. He doesn't pair his socks, him. I watched him at the whirligigs.

Why did I say Steve?

ELLE. Ahh no, not that Steve, another Steve.

I eyeball the chicken basket ont side.

Stev… en… Basket.

MUM. Oh, Steven Basket? Never heard of him?

Steven Basket?! What am I doing?!

Me and Mam never lie to each other. Never. We're upfront. Blunt.

MUM. Well, I'm dead happy for ya Danielle. It's made my week seeing that smile. You can pack it in wit whistling tho.

She grabs my nose and waggles it – like she did when I were a kid.

I feel like pure shit for lying to her. She believes me an' all.

Steven fucking Basket.

MUM. Invite him over then. This Steven Basket, next week. I'll do a lasagne. Hang on, he's not one of those bloody vegans is he?

–

Another week gone.

Work's fine.

Eve's fine.

Things are fine.

We just act normal. In fact, nothing has changed at all.

We haven't talked about it.

Even mentioned it to each other.

But.

We know it happened.

We both have these nuggets – see. Inside.

Right now.

That's enough.

> THE SAME Reprise
> It's all the same,
> Every day.
> It's all the same,
> Round our way.

It's like nothing ever happened actually.

Like that night – that moment never happened.

But it did.

And ever since that night. That moment. That nugget here has changed everything and I literally can't go back to how it was, it's impossible.

I feel like I'm going to explode if I don't talk about it.

If WE don't talk about it –

> Why change?
> When it works this way?
> Why change?
> I like the same.

–

AARON. Oi oi bellends!

Eve and Aaron are 'off'.

They were never actually 'on'. They only ever kissed – that night at Megabowl. She let him down gently. Said she likes him as a friend.

AARON. Got loadsa birds lined up already mate – got em queueing round bend!

All that's just pretend. He proper had the feels. See – All this carpet-carrying malarky is just not real.

A storm blew.

That storm was you.

You rattled my cage,

It wasn't the same since the day I met you.

If the walls fell,

Would you stay put, Elle?

Would you hang on to the ruins as they fell?

Another week crawls by.

It's gone weird.

She's acting different.

And so am I.

I don't know how to be.

How to talk to her any more.

Whether to laugh or joke or…

We're alone.

Do I say something?

If I'm honest –

I wanna do it again.

Kiss her again.

–

AMY. Errr – girls? Come 'ere – I need some boy advice?
You know I've been seeing that lad called Ryan, right?
Girls – I'm smitten. Like, what do I even do?

We've only been going for like two week but I think I
wanna make it offish. But I don't wanna ask 'Will you be
me boyfriend?' Coz that's weeny ladgin int it?

I know I need to chill me bean. But you know that
feeling? Dya know the one I mean? Like you might be
sick – but really good sick? When he texts me, or I hear
his ped – my stomach just flips.

ELLE. Erm – keep it chill Amy mate. Two week int that long.

Is it still the same?
Or have things changed?
This might sound strange –
But I'm glad you came...

Does she hate me?

Have I done something wrong?

Did I force it on her?

I can't work it out and I can't talk to no one.

No one else would get it.

My mam thinks she's 'Steven fucking Basket'.

–

That scary-as-shit but majestic nugget has now fallen into the
pit of my stomach and I can't digest it.

I feel sick.

Sick at the thought of it.

Sick at the thought it might never happen again.

That that was it.

Over – Finished – The end.

–

I do the only thing I know how.

I write her a song…

FOR EVE

You've got an excellent face,

That's what I thought when I first saw you.

You had a freckle on your chin,

But it fell off when I next saw you.

You're funny,

You're kind,

Out of ten – I'd say you're a five…

I'm joking,

You're belting

You're at least a ten point nine.

Look, I know the other night it kicked off,

And to be honest, I didn't want it to stop.

But listen clearly, I swear,

It can all stop right there.

But let's talk.

Let's walk it off.

I'd rather have you in my life as friend, than not.

Coz since I met you, you've changed my view,

I watched the clouds change but I never changed too.

You can be anything you want in the whole wide world
really, can't you?

So thank you.

Did I mention you're really fit too?

      And your kiss is a TEN OUT OF TEN.
      If you want, we can do it again?

Record it.

On my phone.

It's grainy, and a bit shit,

But she'll get the gist.

–

I send it.

Silence – a beat – a moment.

Probably a good place for the interval there int it?

And I need some Dutch courage for this next bit.

–

So – Get a round in, have a smoke – have a stand – have a sit...

I'll see you lovely lot in a bit.

End of Act One

ACT TWO

ELLE *enters*.

Now then! Welcome back!

I hope no one's done a runner?

An interval flit?

A French exit?

Legged it?

Some people do do a runner in the interval don't they?

Put your hand up if you ever have?!

See.

You're all bastards!

–

Right – Remember where we were?

I'd just sent her a recording – a text.

She replied.

Sent me her address.

–

–

Here I am.

Here we are.

Out west.

Not been up this way in years.

I always wondered if you could see Cloudrise from up here.

You can't.

You can hear nature tho. Loud. Loads of it.

Crickets. Badgers? Voles? No cars – no sirens, like a different planet.

–

There's a gate.

And a long drive.

You know like in the films?

You can see the house.

But before the house, there's a gate.

And a long drive.

I'm nervous, can you tell?

.

What's she gonna say? Are her family going to be in? Is this 'meet the parents'? Or is she gonna drown me in her jacuzzi!?

She said turn up after nine… It's half past. I don't wanna be keen like.

I buzz the Dalek-looking thing ont gate. There's a camera. I'm really self-conscious all of a sudden.

(*Distorted female voice.*) Hello.

Is that her? Could be her? Could be her mam? Could be one of her sisters?

ELLE (*coughs*). Hiya. Hello. Is Eve… in?

The gates open. Slow. Electric. Noisy as fuck.

I have this image of lasers and Doberman, but there aren't any.

Stones – pebbles, clatter under my feet. There's about five, maybe six cars to the right and I swear I just saw a horse!

Her house is massive. More long than tall tho... Like Cloudrise, but fallen over on its side.

There's fairy lights. A tree shaped like a – squirrel. A pathway that leads to a swing. Like a whole bench that swings.

.

The more I look, the more I see.

Bit like when you look at stars int it?

When you look up, they grow.

.

I'm suddenly regretting this.

We shoulda just met in Costa or something?

.

The front door swings open. Light floods out.

There she is.

–

Posh hair.

Top knot.

Hands hiding in her pockets.

Joggers and a hoodie.

Bare feet.

–

I've never seen her like this.

But I like it. I think.

EVE. Hi – Well, come in – It's freezing out there!

It's not cold. That was an awkward 'I don't know what to say' thing to say.

The door slams – behind me – shut.

ELLE (*jumps*). 'kin hell.

> As if I just swore?! As if the first words out my mouth were ''kin hell' thru her door.

EVE. You… erm… You found it then?

ELLE. Bit hard to miss to be fair. Have you got a horse?

> Inside looks like a chocolate box. All red drapes and wooden beams. Paintings on the walls of old people – sitting. A piano. Muddy welly boots. A table with about twenty chairs around it.

> There are books. Fucking. Everywhere. You know in *Beauty and the Beast*? The library? Yeah? Bit like that.

EVE. Come thru to the sitting room. Can I get you a drink? We've no beer I'm afraid. But we have gin, vodka, vermouth, whiskey, wine?

> What the fuck's vermouth?

ELLE. Whatever you're having's fine. Should I take me shoes off?

> She's gone. Just like that.

> Leaving me stranded in this gigantic room the size of my entire flat. The carpet's like fresh snow. Dead deep.

> I take me shoes off.

> Just in case, you know? Don't want her family thinking I'm a scruff. And it feels nice doesn't it? Good carpet.

> –

> We sit. Plumped sofas, bare brick, books. Piled up.

> I look out of place.

> Both of us with a goldfish bowl of gin, with basically a garden bush in it.

> I take the shrubbery out and sniff it.

EVE. Rosemary. It's rosemary. From Mum's herb garden.

ELLE. Yeah? Rosemary? Nice one.

Tastes weird.

EVE. Thanks for coming over Elle. They've gone away for the weekend. The family. So... erm... I've got the place to myself.

ELLE. Cool. Nice one. Nice place by the way. I wasn't expecting... Well I don't know what I was expecting but I wasn't expecting... Have you got a horse?

She laughs. We laugh.

EVE. Elle I'm sorry. For how I've been recently. I really am. I'm embarrassed about the way I've... erm... I just haven't known how to be, or what to say or...

She puts her hand on my arm.

Nice. Like ice. Nice ice.

I put my hand on hers. She's as soft as silk, like.

ELLE. I know. Me either. And don't apologise.

Our hands sit. Together. Still.

EVE. I haven't known how to be, what to say, since... Whether to say anything, do anything... I've never... I don't know, I've never been in this situation before... That's the first time I've ever... erm...

I want her to say it. Out loud. It would make it more real if she says it.

...erm... first time I've ever kissed a girl. So...

I squeeze her hand. She squeezes back.

ELLE. Yeah. Me too.

Fingertips touch. Palms come together.

EVE. And your gig, and how you played, and how we talked...

Fingers interlace, slide between each other.

EVE. I felt… I feel connected to you in a way I've never known. There's something about you, I just…

A surge of electricity – Like fingers in the mains, a chemical reaction, a rush of blood thru our veins to our brains.

Our hands.

One rough – One soft.

There's no going back if this lid comes off…

EVE. Shit, I can't believe this is coming out of my mouth…

She has an excellent mouth.

Fuck me, like a really excellent gob.

And before she carries on – that lid comes off.

I kiss her.

Fuck it.

It's like a magnet.

Like the moon pulls the sea.

Like a wave from the deepest depths of me.

We kiss like we want to climb into each other. We kiss like we wanna wear each other's skins. We kiss until I forget what my face feels like without her on it.

–

She grabs my hand, pulls me up.

We stagger thru a labyrinth of books.

Pass paintings full of vacant faces.

Family photos – her parents give me looks.

She opens her bedroom door.

We stumble in.

PURE

Pure ecstasy,
Her body climbing up on top of me,
Her fingers loosely clutching to mine.

Pure chemistry,
Goosebumps all over bodies,
Hearts pounding at the same time.

Pure recklessly,
She grabs every little bit of me,
There's fire building inside.

We lose our clothes and lay together,
I trace her shape
and I have never
felt another woman this way.

(Middle 8)
I want you, it's falling out of me,
Like an ocean, I'm drowning in your sea.
Her tidal wave is falling over me,
I can't help it, I can't help it.

CHORUS
I'm free
I'm free
I've never done this before,
But I feels so pure.

–

We lose our breath,
we lay together,
She shakes all over and I have never,

Made another woman feel this way.

CHORUS
We're free,
We're free,
Just her and me – Drowning in our sea,
I've never done this before,
But I'd do it a million times more…

It feels so normal. So natural. Like the easiest thing I've ever done.

Maybe coz we're both lasses we skipped the awkward bit? The bit where you aren't sure what does what? But it was like I'd done it a million times before – In a previous life or something.

–

She has freckles on her stomach – Real ones. I draw them, dot to dot. 'Take her and cut her out in little stars…' Like constellations in the sky.

She has a birthmark on her thigh that's shaped a bit like Australia.

I don't want to stare.

But she is beautiful.

YOU AND ME
There's a cloud in the sky that is shaped exactly like your eyes,
It's a clear day it's true,
But the sky somehow looks a bit like you.
It seems to me, it's a crazy idea but I'm crazy it seems,
That everywhere I go,
There's a little bit of you just letting me know that you're, that you're still around…

Me and Eve have been inseparable since 'That night'.

Obsessed.

We try not to make it obvious to anyone.

Coz. Well. It'd be a mess.

This summer is HOT.

Proper hot.

The tarmac melts down our way.

The odd cloud pokes its nose in to see what's going on. But mainly Cloudrise swims in a haze of turquoise.

–

We snatch every moment we can find.

A cheeky arse-squeeze, a sly kiss. She whispers that she wants to… And we do.

I tell her I'm literally obsessed with the way her collarbones just sit there. Like bike handles.

As I walk, thru the city.

There's a homeless man, whistling a ditty.

It reminds me of that song that we played, those clarinet days.

I drop him some change, and I carry on walking and I feel a bit strange, that you just pop into my brain. Yeah it keeps on happening every day. Count down the hours.

Till I see your face.

We do loads of mint stuff, I could reel off a list.

But it's a bit smug that innit? And even the un-mint stuff is mint with Eve.

Oh – by the way. She does have a horse.

Knew it.

'Darcy.'

She showed me.

Rode it.

Asked me if I wanted a go, but I'm not a fan of horses to be fair.

CHORUS

You and me, we should be together
Coz when I'm with you
You make me lighter than a feather.

–

I meet her family.

EVE. And this is my friend, Elle.

They do BBQs, all Waitrose of course – sit round on huge picnic blankets popping corks.

Tried my first prawn. The ones you have to rip its head off and dissect.

They're nice actually.

Her 'daddy' is a bit of prick, but her mam is hilarious!

She smokes like a chimney, pretty much pissed all the time,

EVE'S MAM. Dahhrling Elle… I've heard you've got a very beautiful voice.

Eve would roll her eyes at her. But I like her. She reminds me of Patsy from – what's it called…?

You and me we should be together,
Together in each other's arms all day, every day, come rain or shine I have to say,
Since I met you – I can't shake you.
Yes it's true,
It should be me and you.

I stay over sometimes too, well – quite a lot actually.

When it comes to sleeping arrangements, I'm in the spare room.

Never sleep in it tho.

But I ruffle the covers so it looks like I have.

I creep out, dead of night –

We lie in bed. And it isn't always… Sometimes – we just talk.

–

EVE. Sometimes I wish we could swap. You know…? Life swap.

ELLE. Ahh shit off.

EVE. It's just… it's not all it's cracked up to be this, you know Elle? I wish I was free. I wish I could just… be. Whoever, whatever I wanted to be.

ELLE. You can be… you can do anything? You taught me that…

EVE. …Just so much is expected you know? So much. Go to university. Study medicine. Find a husband. Have children.

ELLE. Right? Well… what dya wanna do?

EVE. I want… I want to paint. I want to learn how to make little origami boats from paper. I want to throw a dart at a map and go there. Tomorrow. With you. I want to walk dogs for a living. Or comb cats with long hair. I want to count all the stars in the sky. Name them all. I want to walk on a beach holding your hand and not worry about a thing. I want to not worry about a thing. I want to… I want to talk to my mum – about anything, and for her to remember the conversation in the morning. I want… I want to be me.

–

Week later.

I bring her to Cloudrise.

I'm nervous at first.

Dunno why.

Well I do.

Because she's got a fucking river running thru her garden and we've only got four rooms.

Mam's confused by her at first, she's cautious of people sometimes, me mam.

MAM. She's very nice this Eve? But can you let me know when she's coming over next? I need to hoover.

I'm proud to show her Cloudrise. The views out my bedroom window blow her mind. We put on Dad's vinyl, coz she asks. She remembers.

–

The sky is dead pretty like.

I stand behind her – arms wrapped round her – Like Simba and Mufasa.

Show her what her ends look like from up high.

–

I wish so hard it was quiet, no noise – just us.

But I can hear knobhead neighbour upstairs hoovering, his music thuds. Eve laughs, says it sounds like the ceiling's caving in.

She's right, you know? It's so small here – so hemmed in.

That's the thing – These walls are paper thin.

See I – I wanna soak up every – second of her being here. But I can't relax – I can't – We whisper chats, pillows drown out sound. At Eve's house, no one's ever around. Floors and doors separate us all. But my mam's right there, her headboard against my wall.

It's alright tho – coz Eve's here. With her guacamole-greens and her little ears.

We wake up early and watch the sun rise.

I get her favourite cereal in.

Crunchy Nut.

CHORUS
You and me, we should be together
Coz when I hold your hand
I wanna hold it forever.
You and Me, Elle and Eve –
Impossible to find the words but I've some up my sleeve,
Swear down you're mint, I'd put your name in bold print.
I'd buy you a car if I wasn't skint.
You're amazing, feel like you're a daydream.
It's true,
Eve I think I...

See what I did there?!

Stopped myself.

Before I get too carried away.

Don't wanna regret anything I say.

One time tho, middle of the night. We'd just had sex. So close, tangled together and I couldn't feel my legs.

It was like she said it. Those three words. But... Without the words. I thought she was gonna for a second – you know – say it. She didn't... but I felt it.

I wanna tell EVERYONE – Me mam, Shitbrick, Jack.

But it just isn't that easy. People are scared of things that are different – Things they don't understand. It's the stuff people say – You know? The daily chat – the shitty, narky comments and nobody reacts.

People keep schtum, don't speak up – but if I'm blunt – I do it too. I keep my mouth shut.

All the times I've...

It's ugly – it's within me and I feel proper tight. But it's easier just to let things go, than say owt, right?

The other day after work, we're hiding round the back. Dead close, cuddling, this lad rocks up. I think it's Jack.

It's not.

He comes around the corner just as I lean in to kiss her. She throws me off, panics – Says I'm her sister.

Boys, lads, men. Comments, night and day –

Going to hold hands in public and us both pulling away.

Even my brother – Shitbrick – thinks she's fit, he text me 'Is she single? Can I have her number?'

Prick...

Basically – It's shit.

And it's hard to lie about something that makes you so happy int it?

–

MAM. Gobshiiite!

ELLE. What?!

MAM. Were you born in a barn?!

She should know. She were there.

ELLE. You should know – you were there!

MAM. Smart arse! Front door's wide open!

ELLE. It's red hot. It's too stuffy in here. I'm tryna get some air thru!

Me and mam drift apart over the last few week. Guess coz I'm spending so much time with Eve. At Eve's house. Mam's got the sads recently too. So I feel extra bad.

ELLE. You alright then?

MAM. Fine bab. Whack telly on would ya. *Chase* **is on.**

She plonks down ont sofa – Sighs her lungs empty – puts her feet up.

I just stare at her for a bit.

I think about telling her. Maybe. Imagine. Telling her. Everything.

About Eve. About how happy I am. About how my heart goes mental when I see her. The way we hold hands when we sleep – like otters. About how much we laughed last weekend she wee'd herself. About how she's the first thing I think about, and last thing at night. About how meeting her and her family, I'd peeked through so many new doors I want to explore some more. I realise there's a whole world out there, opportunities galore, and I've only seen this tiny corner of it before. About how she's leaving soon. About how she's leaving. And we're both just ignoring it. About how I think I'm in love with her.

I think I am, you know? In love.

–

ELLE. Good day then?

MAM. Ooh, am bloody jiggered love.

.

I could just tell her?

Sat here with our brews in front of Bradley Walsh.

We share everything, me and Mam.

Even the same bath water when I were little.

I want to tell her.

I want her to know.

I'm gonna tell her…

MAM. Oh you'll never believe it? You know the Duffield lads on floor six? Danny? The one with the hair? He's come out as a gay. Doreen told me this morning int stairwell. That's two of em now. Out of six. God. Bet their mam wonders what she's done wrong…

She continues watching The Chase.

Queen Victoria – b… press it then! – Yes, knew it.

Won't be telling her today then.

–

Eve's leaving tomorrow.

Time's flown. I tried to make it slow down – but it just goes.

Today's Eve's last shift at 'Chips and Dips'.

And I'm gonna soak up every second of her and it.

I wake her up early and surprise her. Take her for breakfast to this café I'd heard of out of town.

Give her a croggy on my bike.

Her arms wrapped round me from behind – tight.

No one knows us round here, so we'll be safe.

You know – Out of sight.

It's quite posh. This café, you know?

We have coffee, in a pot. Bottled water, not tap.

I have ham and eggs – eggs 'benedick' they call it?

She has kedgeree. Which I can't get my head round? Fish and rice? In a morning? No thanks.

We talk, it's what we do best.

And laugh.

Laugh about daft stuff.

Like the waiter's squeaky shoes.

But I feel sick...
There's this voice in my head this tick tock tick.
It's like sand falling thru my fingers. Tryna make it stop.
Wish I could just press pause like on Bernard's watch.

We don't talk about the obvious.

We don't broach the subject of her leaving.

We don't talk plans of what to do next.

Or what 'this' even is.

We just exist.

In the now.

And the now is …

Not enough. Why don't we just talk?

About this fucking elephant in the room?

About how we are made for each other and soon –

soon it'll be over and then what do we do?

Breakfast done.

Leave the café.

Leave to get to work early, so no questions will be asked.

We're pros at being sneaky now.

Arrival times – Split…

But I still feel sick.

No.

It's not the eggs 'benedict'

It's…

This is not –

right.

I feel edgy – uptight.

I don't wanna feel like this today.

Our last day, but.

We get to my bike.

I freeze.

I see it – locked up,

chained against some railings.

I feel the same…

Wheels and frame, chained.

Hands and lips – contained.

Her collarbones, like bike handles –

We are running out of time.

And I want to climb on top of every roof and shout 'she's mine.'

–

EVE. Elle – are you okay? You look like you've seen a ghost…

I grab her hand. Hands. Both of em. Soft.

ELLE. I— listen Eve – I – need to—

I need to stop.

But –

her eyes –

guacamole-green.

Honest to god – She's the most beautiful fucking thing I've ever seen.

ELLE. I – Eve… I'm…

I love you.

THEM THREE WORDS
Them three words,
I've never said them before out loud.
And now they've just fallen out my mouth.
There's no going back now.

Then she cries,
Not quite the reaction I had in mind.
Normally you get it said back or they at least smile.
She holds her face in her hands for a while.

It gets awkward quick.

Time ticking.

The air thickening.

Cut it with a knife it'd ooze out sizzling.

Then she speaks,
Her voice comes out croaky – kinda weak.
She coughs and wipes her cheek.
Then she says something I wish she didn't mean...
You're my best friend...
You're my best friend...
I'm her best fucking friend.

Back ont bike, it starts to rain –

Her arms wrapped round me from behind again, tears rolling down my face.

I wish she'd get the fuck off me – but – not – too.

Fuck—

This pain man,

this pain.

–

I'm questioning my own mind –

My own sanity.

All the hugging, touching, coming, clutching, buzzing, rushing, loving –

Was never actually a reality?

> From the horse's mouth,
> This girl came up north from the south, turned everything upside down.
> Now I don't know,
> Was any of it real? Or just for show?
> I'll wear it as badge of honour clearly,
> I'll sign off yours sincerely,
> Your best fucking friend don't you know?

Chips and Dips.

Spin in. Lock up.

We don't stagger entrances.

I couldn't give a fuck.

'Best friends'?!

Well, sorry Eve, soz 'mate'. Sorry for the mistake. I don't normally lie naked, tracing the curves of my mates.

Wipe my eyes.

Walk in.

AARON. Oi oi – here they are! The 'dirty fucking dykes'.

–

Have I walked into a bad dream?

Did he just say what I think he did…

–

You two been munching muff have you? That why you're late? What?! You think we've haven't noticed…?! It's fucking obvious mate. It's just not fucking normal – lesbians? You make me sick – thing is right, you just haven't had the right dick…

I look at Eve, she's gone pure white. Then suddenly – out the corner of my eye…

Jack is on the attack – launches himself at Aaron. Fists bare.

He smacks him straight across the jaw – about there…

Aaron flies – lands on his back, as he's mid air he knocks an entire day's worth of dips on the kitchen floor – smashed.

–

Houmous – ketchup, flying.

Punches – headbutts, diving.

Eddie – silent.

Amy – in shock.

Barry – erupting flames – head about to blow off.

–

BARRY. Cut it out boyos! Stop right there! Jack – Aaron. My office now.

A moment – silence – a beat

AMY. Ohmygod – Are you two shagging?! That's amazing! I love lesbians! Like, I don't know any… but I love Sue Perkins off the telly. I wouldn't have thought you two were tho – you know – lezzas? Coz you've got long hair and that…

But Elle, mate – whatthefuck – you don't fancy me dya?

Maybe I'm a bit… you know? – Coz – well I always loved Xena Warrior Princess growing up – but I dunno.

No.

No.

I could never – actually –

Ugh. No.

No offence!

But like, come on then? Is it true?!

If you don't mind me asking? What do you actually do?

Eve grabs my hand. Tight. We walk out.

–

It's hot again.

Sun back out.

Pavement wet and steaming from the clouds spurting out.

Busy out.

–

Neither of us talking.

Just walking.

Holding hands.

I'd forgot we were actually.

Holding hands.

It's confusing.

We'd never done it in public before.

Maybe now we are 'just friends' it doesn't matter any more?

She's squeezing so tightly I've lost the feeling in my little finger.

There's a bench.

We stop.

We sit.

I look up.

There's a rainbow.

I squeeze her hand to look up –

but she lets it go.

–

My heart shatters into a thousand and one pieces.

–

EVE. Elle – I erm… listen I – I didn't want it to end this way? I didn't want anyone to find out? But… you do know we are just friends, Elle? Just. Friends. Having. Fun. You didn't actually think it would – carry on?

ELLE. I don't…

I…

Just…

What did you want me to think, Eve?

You started this –

You kissed me after my gig.

You…

You invited me to your house and we did… what we did

you..

You grabbed me… you you you you.

And now it's all my fault for reading in to it right…?

Right…

I wish… I fucking… wish I could wash my brain out – I wish I'd never fucking met you then I wouldn't have to feel owt.

Fuck – you. You rock up here with your… your big house and your fresh kicks and kiss me like you did – pick me up and drop me when it suits?! Yeah – of course – but that's what you do, int it? Yeah? When things get too big for you – you just do what your daddy tells you to do? What he thinks is best for you?

What did you say that night? Go to university – find a husband – have children, right? Well knock yourself out and do that then!

I –

I fucking…

I know you. I know you don't want all that.

You've gotta live your life – you know that? Not them. They'll be fucking dead one day and what then?!

You –

You can't do this – to people – do whatever you… want.

You can't just take from people the bits you benefit from.

You disgust me, you fucking dyke, you know that?

–

MAM. Gobshiiite.

ELLE. I'm fine!

I decide not to go back to Chips and Dips.

Missed call after missed call.

Text after text.

Ignore it all.

She's been gone a month.

NOBODY HEARD

Busy street, fast moving feet.

Tired eyes, zero sleep.

The green man flashes in my eyes tonight.

Reflection there, but no soul found.

Time to blend into the crowd.

Watch the world pass me by...

CHORUS

Do you ever feel lonely when there's a thousand people around?

Could you see my face and hold my gaze, and notice me in a crowd?

Do you remember the time you caught my eye, and told me you were in love?

Without the words?

Don't worry, nobody heard.

So here I am back to the start.

Thought I knew myself, then I fell apart.

It was all the same till you showed up.

You've pecked my head,

I've lost my way,

I was doing fine now I'm not okay.

Can we reverse back to the good old days?

CHORUS

Do you ever feel lonely when there's a thousand people around?

Could you see my face and hold my gaze, and notice me in a crowd?

Do you remember the time you caught my eye, and told me you were in love?

Without the words?

Don't worry, nobody heard.

> Except me...
> Except me...
> Except me...

Turns out being heartbroken makes you write a lot of songs.

Since Eve's gone, songs are falling out my head like Skittles in them adverts. I know I've said that twice.

–

I'm not coping good if I'm honest.

Everything I see, every song I hear – write – every fucking TREE reminds me of her.

I start eating pink wafers.

I smell her smell down the street, think I'm gonna turn round and she'll be there. And hold me.

I dream about her – which really fucks up your day doesn't it?

I saw a whoopee cushion on Tuesday and cried.

Cried.

Coz of a whoopee cushion.

Keep thinking about my dad. Talking to him a bit – sounds mad that don't it? But... safe innit. Dunno how he'd react if he were here – but he'd know something were up. He wouldn't say owt – but he'd probably force me to listen to some... Leonard Cohen or summat.

Can't talk to anyone. Anyone alive anyway –

I've kinda shut off. Closed off, phone on silent and shut up shop...

But it's rising – Up to here – Choking me a bit.

Mam's worried. So on my case that I tell her 'StevenfuckingBasket's binned me off.

That's shut her up for a bit.

I get a cleaning job at a school down't road.

Also, I've not told anyone but –

I've applied to some music colleges.

Stupid really.

Not heard owt back so… we'll see.

That's one thing I can thank her for I guess.

Eve.

I think why not, why not eh?

I could give it a go.

I put on her 'quiet confidence' like sheep in wolf's clothes.

–

I haven't heard from her. Not a peep. Not at all. Dunno what I expected after what I said but – I thought she might call… or text.

Don't even know if she got there safe.

I wanna ask her what Oxford's like?

Has been on a punt? She told me about them.

Does everyone in Oxford wear socks and sandals?

But no. Nowt.

You know, even if we are 'just friends'… 'Best Friends' apparently, you'd call? Or text? Wouldn't you?

–

It's Friday.

I think.

My phone rings. It's on silent. But I see it.

–

It's Jack?

–

I ignore it.

–

Rings again.

Jack…

–

Arr Jack isn't the kind of bloke to ring up out the blue.
Specially twice?

ELLE *hesitates to answer, she answers.*

ELLE. Hello..?

JACK. Now then.

ELLE. You alright mate?

JACK. Yep. Are you?

ELLE. Yeah fine pal…

–

–

ELLE. Is there something wrong, Jack or…

–

JACK. Now, I just want you to know.

I know.

And I don't just mean about you and Eve.

I mean about yous. I know.

I'm sorry you're going thru this on your own mate.

If you wanna talk 'bout it, I'm here.

**If you wanna tell me to fuck off and never mention it
again. That's cool too.**

But it's okay, you know?

I get it. I've got you.

What you two had was special.

She was special.

But so are you Elle…

You don't have to hide who you really are.

I've got your back.

–

… You there mate?

ELLE *pulls the phone away from her ear,*
she looks at the handset.

To talk or not to talk.

She puts phone back to her ear,
breathes in deeply to begin to talk…

The End (–ish).

We are back in the beginning 'gig format'.

ELLE *addresses the audience in real time.*

So this, that, what you've just heard was me – ten-ish year
ago.

Shitloads has happened since then.

I got into music college in London. Get me! Ooh err! Moved
to London for a bit, then to Leeds, then to Manchester. Never
stay anywhere for too long.

I float.

Like a cloud, I guess.

But Cloudrise. Cloudrise will always be home.

I miss it.

–

Erm, what else?

Oh yeah, I'm a lesbian. A big ole gay! Out and proud.

Once Jack had knocked on my closet there was no turning back.

It was hard – Not gonna lie. And it takes time.

Some folk were sound, some were pricks. My mam – took it pretty bad and that was shit. That was the bleakest thing of all, really.

Things were said that are hard to forget – Like she's glad me da int around no more, coz he'd be disappointed.

Look – I don't want tiny violins or owt – I guess I just want folk to know it's not easy coming out. It's a journey – for everyone – and now it's fine.

But the censoring.

Of anything.

Of anyone.

Of yourself.

Of someone else.

Is exhausting and it cuts you open from the inside.

Don't do it to yourself, or anyone else. I beg you.

In the darkest time – I found my light. My tribe, my pals for life.

My chosen family –

They know who they are.

I'd write 'An Ode to My Pals', but that's going a bit far!

–

I still gig, I still swear too much, and I get paid to do this kinda shit for a living.

I never thought – dreamed this life would be mine.

And I still thank Eve for that.

–

Right…

Now Eve.

Suppose you're wondering what happened there? Where is she? What was her fucking problem?!

Well, I didn't hear from her. At all.

Not a dickie bird.

Until June 7th, 2019.

No, I'm not Rainman – I just remember the date because I was back for Mam's birthday. Back at Cloudrise.

We've gone to her favourite Italian – for pizza and tira-mee-suu. Then to the local for some jars and karaoke. And of course Mam's made me go up and sing her favourite song 'Jolene'.

I hate karaoke by the way, but it is Mam's birthday – So I have to or there's no speaking to her.

The intro starts, when my phone rings in my pocket.

Vibrates.

Give it a quick check before I blast out some Dolly.

EVE

Calling.

I shit you not.

Eve.

What the fuck?!

I didn't even know I had her number still!

I pocket it.

Start singing…

–

I had that feeling where the air's been sucked out the room again.

Head all hot again.

Feel sick as a dog again.

–

Eve?

It's been ten years.

Ten fucking years.

What's she playing at?

–

Song over. Few claps, cheers.

Trying to get back to my beer.

Get stopped on the way, chatted to, by folks I've barely ever spoken to.

'How's the music going you? Have you been on *X Factor* yet?'

'How's that London? Are your bogeys black?'

'Have you got a boyfriend?'

My phone burning a hole in my pocket.

I nod, smile – chicane thru the crowd.

I make it outside.

So quiet – no sound.

Look sideways.

Both ways.

No one there.

Happy days.

.

Phone out.

Kinda don't want to look.

Missed call.

…

One voicemail message.

Now before I listen…

We listen…

The thought of her still hurts my heart, you know?

I've moved on.

Of course.

It's been ten years – I'm not a nun!

I've had my fair share of girlfriends – Some good, some bad,
some hardly worth a mention.

But there's always that one person, isn't there? That never
really goes away…

–

Ten years Eve?

Ten out of ten.

Ten men.

Ten for the 'win'.

She plays the voicemail.

It is the actual voice of Eve.

EVE. Hi.

Elle?

Erm…

It's Eve.

I'm not sure if this is your number still?

But yes,

It's Eve – Evelyn here – Eve.

Erm…

.

I came across your number in my phone.

And, erm…

I had to call.

.

To be honest, I should have called you much earlier.
Probably, ten years earlier, really – Unforgivable – sorry –
erm…

.

How are you?!

Gosh, shit – How are you Elle?

I've seen you're doing really well.

That sounds weird and rather stalkerish – sorry – Erm…

But I heard you on the radio last week. And hearing you sing again…

I, Erm – yes…

That's what prompted my call to be honest.

Ever since…

I've not really been able to think of much else.

Anybody else.

Really.

Gosh. Shit.

.

I'm so SO glad you're doing what you're doing. Fulfilling your…

I mean I knew you were always bloody brilliant and rather bloody marvellous – in every way, but to see you…

Erm… I'm rambling – Sorry – Nervous – Silly.

–

I'm still in Oxford. I'm a doctor. Can… erm… tick that off the list!

I've got two little ones with – John my, erm.

Been married two years now. So.

.

.

I still think of you a lot Elle.

I still think about our time. Together. That summer. I – Do you remember when I came to that fancy-dress party as a whoopee cushion?! I mean what was I thinking…!?

Eve releases a large out-breath, a sigh.

The rest of the call is more measured, more considered.

I want to thank you.

Really.

.

It was… You were… Perfect.

I just…

I just…

.

couldn't.

.

.

And I never told you.

I never said it back.

That day – With the rainbow.

I love you too.

I did.

I do.

And I forever will.

It is as if a huge weight has been lifted from her chest.

Crazy all this really, isn't it?!

Ten years!

Anyway,

Yes. Erm…

Thank you.

.

.

Bloody hell…

She hangs up.

The End.

A Nick Hern Book

Bloody Elle first published in Great Britain as a paperback original in 2021 by Nick Hern Books Limited, The Glasshouse, 49a Goldhawk Road, London W12 8QP

Bloody Elle copyright © 2021 Lauryn Redding

Lauryn Redding has asserted her right to be identified as the author of this work

Cover photograph by Pippa Rankin

Designed and typeset by Nick Hern Books, London
Printed in Great Britain by Mimeo Ltd, Huntingdon, Cambridgeshire PE29 6XX

A CIP catalogue record for this book is available from the British Library

ISBN 978 1 83904 020 7

Woodland
CARBON
www.woodlandcarbon.co.uk
NICK HERN BOOKS
Printed on Carbon Captured paper

www.nickhernbooks.co.uk

facebook.com/nickhernbooks

twitter.com/nickhernbooks